Lord Mountbatten

Josephine Ross

Illustrated by
Peter Gregory

Hamish Hamilton

Titles in the Profiles *series*

Muhammad Ali	0-241-10600-1	Kevin Keegan	0-241-10594-3
Chris Bonington	0-241-11044-0	Helen Keller	0-241-11295-8
Ian Botham	0-241-11031-9	Martin Luther King	0-241-10931-0
Geoffrey Boycott	0-241-10712-1	Paul McCartney	0-241-10930-2
Charlie Chaplin	0-241-10479-3	Lord Mountbatten	0-241-10593-5
Winston Churchill	0-241-10482-3	Rudolf Nureyev	0-241-10849-7
Sebastian Coe	0-241-10848-9	Pope John Paul II	0-241-10711-3
Roald Dahl	0-241-11043-2	Anna Pavlova	0-241-10481-5
Thomas Edison	0-241-10713-X	Prince Philip	0-241-11167-6
Queen Elizabeth II	0-241-10850-0	Lucinda Prior-Palmer	0-241-10710-5
The Queen Mother	0-241-11030-0	Barry Sheene	0-241-10851-9
Alexander Fleming	0-241-11203-6	Mother Teresa	0-241-10933-7
Anne Frank	0-241-11294-X	Margaret Thatcher	0-241-10596-X
Gandhi	0-241-11166-8	Daley Thompson	0-241-10932-9
Basil Hume	0-241-11204-4	Queen Victoria	0-241-10480-7

First published 1981 by
Hamish Hamilton Children's Books
Garden House, 57-59 Long Acre, London WC2E 9JZ
© text 1981 by Hamish Hamilton Ltd
© illustrations 1981 Hamish Hamilton Ltd
Reprinted 1984
All rights reserved

Cover photograph reproduced
by courtesy of Camera Press

British Library Cataloguing in Publication Data
Ross, Josephine
Mountbatten.
1. Mountbatten, Louis Mountbatten, Earl, 1900-1979
– Juvenile literature
2. Great Britain, Royal Navy – Biography
– Juvenile literature
3. Viceroys – India – Biography
– Juvenile literature
941.082′092′4   DA89.1.M59
ISBN 0-241-10593-5

Typeset by Pioneer
Printed in Great Britain at the
University Press, Cambridge

Contents

1	'A BEAUTIFUL LARGE CHILD'	5
2	THE SAILOR PRINCE	9
3	IN TIME OF PEACE	17
4	THE SINKING OF THE *KELLY*	26
5	IN TIME OF WAR	32
6	SUPREMO	36
7	THE LAST VICEROY	42
8	FIRST SEA LORD	48
9	DEATH OF A HERO	55
	Important events in Lord Mountbatten's life	62

1 'A Beautiful Large Child'

On a June morning at the beginning of this century a small notice appeared in *The Times*. 'Princess Louis of Battenberg yesterday morning gave birth to a son at Frogmore Lodge, Windsor Castle', it announced. 'Both the Princess and the child are doing well.'

It did not seem a very important event at the time. Yet as the 20th century unfolded, this boy was to become one of the greatest figures in modern British history — military commander, Admiral of the Fleet, social leader, and for a while, 'probably the most powerful man in the world', the last ruler of imperial India. When he died, killed by an IRA bomb, he would be mourned by millions. But on 25 June 1900, when he was born, the future Earl Mountbatten of Burma was merely the fourth child of one of Queen Victoria's many granddaughters, the newest member of a very large royal family.

His state funeral in 1979 was televised to the nation, but his christening in the summer of 1900 was a small private ceremony, held in the drawing-room at Frogmore, where his parents were staying. Queen Victoria, then a stout, short-sighted old lady of 81, was godmother, and she held the baby during the service. According to a family story he cried loudly and knocked off her spectacles, but she was delighted with her latest great-grandson, whom she described as 'a beautiful large child'.

To please the elderly Queen, the baby was christened Albert, after her beloved husband, followed by the names Victor Nicholas Louis Francis. Officially he was to be known as Prince Louis of Battenberg, like his father, but a nickname was quickly found for him, and it stuck; to his family and friends he would always be just 'Dickie'.

For a royal child Dickie had an unusual upbringing. His father, a German prince of the illustrious House of Hesse, loved England so much that he had left his own country to join the British navy. So Dickie, with his older brother George and sisters Alice and Louise, was brought up to the Forces life, sometimes living in London, when Prince Louis was based at the Admiralty, at other times moving about the world to Malta, Gibraltar or Venice, or wherever their father's career took them. Some of Dickie's earliest memories were of battleships and foreign places.

As a boy he hero-worshipped his father, but the strongest influence on him during his childhood was his mother. Princess Louis of Battenberg — born the Princess Victoria, daughter of Queen Victoria's daughter Alice and the Grand Duke Louis IV of Hesse and the Rhine — was a woman of intelligence and charm, and Dickie loved her dearly. Though he was the youngest of the family by eight years, his mother saw to it that he did not become either spoilt or lonely. She taught him his lessons, and encouraged his interests in everything from pets to the newly-invented aeroplanes.

By the time he was 10 years old, when he was sent off to boarding school, Dickie was a lively, self-willed boy with a great deal of his mother's charm and a mind that

Dickie at the age of five

was imaginative and alert rather than academic. At his school, Locker's Park in Hertfordshire, he showed no special talent for subjects such as Latin and maths. But he enjoyed history and geography, he spoke fluent German, and he knew more than most boys of his age about world affairs, kings and governments.

There was never any doubt in his mind about what he wanted to do in life. He was going to be a sailor, like his father, and serve in the British navy. It was an exciting prospect for a boy in the early 1900s, when Britain was a great power, with an Empire that stretched across a quarter of the globe. Britannia still ruled the waves — though there were growing signs that Germany, under the ambitious Kaiser William II, was building up her own strength at sea. It was one of the proudest moments of Dickie's life when, just before his thirteenth birthday, he passed through the gates of the Royal Naval College, Osborne, in the Isle of Wight — no longer a child, but a naval Cadet on the threshold of a glorious career.

2 The Sailor Prince

Life at Osborne, as the new Cadet Prince Louis of Battenberg soon discovered, could be tough. His royal connections did not protect him against either bullying or beating, and the fact that his father now held the top naval post of First Sea Lord was no help to young Dickie. But although he was often in fights, and had few close friends, he stood up for himself and managed to keep cheerful.

On one occasion, however, he did make a public complaint. It was a story he loved to tell in later years. Apparently Winston Churchill, who was then the Minister responsible for the navy, came down to Osborne in 1913 to inspect the Cadets. Seeing Dickie, whose father he worked with and knew well, he asked the boy how he was, and if he needed anything. Dickie seized the opportunity to ask if the number of sardines served for supper could in future be increased from two each to three. Churchill promised to see what he could do, but alas, the extra sardines never appeared.

Some of the happiest times of Dickie's boyhood were the summer holidays which he spent abroad, staying with his German and Russian relations. In the fairytale settings of family palaces such as Heiligenberg and

Wolfsgarten, Dickie the English schoolboy turned into Dickie the German prince, whose playmates were Grand Duchesses. Olga, Tatiana, Marie and Anastasia, daughters of the Tsar of Russia, were his first cousins, closer to him in age than his own sisters, and Dickie was very fond of them. With them he played tennis and croquet, and went on expeditions, rides and picnics — and only the prospect of being together again the next year consoled them when the end of the holidays came.

The summer of 1913 was to be the last of these carefree holidays, however. By the following year England and Germany were at war: the armies of one of Queen Victoria's grandsons, King George V, were fighting against the forces of another, the Kaiser William II, in a terrible, wasteful slaughter. For young Dickie, two tragedies in particular would stand out from the horrors of the First World War years. One was the murder of his beloved cousins, the Tsar's daughters, along with their parents and little brother, after the Russian revolution of 1917. The other was the injustice done to his father.

Though Prince Louis of Battenberg was German by birth, his loyalties lay with Britain, where he had lived for most of his life and whose navy he now commanded. Dickie never doubted that he, like his father and older brother George, would fight for Britain in the coming conflict; his only question was whether it would last long enough to allow a junior Cadet such as himself to take part in the action. He had already had a thrilling taste of life on board ship, at the Spithead naval review, when the might of the British navy passed before the King, with bands playing and flags waving, in a fine show that

Dickie's parents, Princess Victoria of Hesse and
Prince Louis of Battenberg

was also a preparation for war. On that occasion Dickie
found himself sharing a cabin in a battlecruiser with his
much-loved brother — now Lieutenant Prince George
of Battenberg — and it increased his longing for the day
when he too would be a naval officer.

Dickie and Prince Louis of Battenberg dined together
at Mall House, the First Sea Lord's official residence, on
the evening of 4 August 1914, the day war broke out. The

11

eager 14-year-old cadet was surprised by his father's air of sadness. He was to understand it all too soon.

There was no quick, knock-out battle at sea, as many others besides young Dickie had hoped. In the first months of the war Germany showed that her navy was at least a match for Britain's, and the newspaper reports told of British cruisers sunk and German commanders triumphant. In such an atmosphere, with patriotism and hatred running high, the public began to look for someone to blame — and with a German prince as First Sea Lord, they had not far to seek.

At Osborne, Dickie did his best to laugh off the jokes against his father, however hurtful words such as 'Hun' and 'spy' might be. But it soon became impossible for Prince Louis to carry on as First Sea Lord in the face of what threatened to become a general campaign against him. With great dignity, he resigned his office, in October 1914.

His father's forced resignation had a deep effect on Dickie. The injustice of it made him sad and angry. It also strengthened his resolve to achieve a brilliant naval career for himself, which would make up for the insult to his father and re-establish the family name. It became Dickie's greatest ambition, which he was to pursue steadfastly for the next forty years, that one day he would fill his father's place in the British navy, as First Sea Lord.

While Prince and Princess Louis retired to live quietly in the Isle of Wight, hiding their distress from public eyes and taking no further official part in the war, Dickie passed out of Osborne and into the Royal Naval College,

Mountbatten (*left*) with his brother George and his father

Dartmouth. He had not yet given much sign of brilliance, although he worked hard; it was not until the last stage of his training, just before going to sea, that he achieved top marks. It was as though he had suddenly realised that his goal was in sight.

To his disappointment, he had missed the great sea-battle of Jutland, though his brother George had been in the thick of it. But the ship in which he was to serve, the *Lion*, had been there, and to complete Dickie's joy, she was the flagship of his hero, Admiral Sir David Beatty.

Now a Midshipman, Dickie began his fighting career in July 1916, in action against the German fleet in the

North Sea. A month later, he again came up against the enemy, and this time he saw some of the terrifying modern weapons in use, including the Zeppelins — German airships — and torpedoes. Dickie was always fascinated by technical inventions and discoveries; he was very much a man of the 20th century.

It was in the darkest year of the war, 1917, that a major change took place in Dickie's life. At a time when anti-German propaganda was reaching its peak, it was considered wise for Prince Louis of Battenberg, along with other members of the royal family, to make a complete break with his foreign past and take a British name. In ceasing to be a German subject he would no longer be a Prince. Instead he was given a specially-created English title — Marquess of Milford Haven. The family surname was translated straight into English — 'berg', the German word for 'hill' or 'mountain', becoming simply 'Mount'. And so the Battenbergs became the Mountbattens.

Victoria Milford Haven, as Dickie's mother was now called, was saddened by the breaking of ties with their past, though styles and titles meant little to her. Dickie, however, enjoyed anything to do with titles, uniforms, decorations and honours. He was now the younger son of an English peer, and in future he would be known as Lord Louis Mountbatten.

By the end of the war his full title was Sub-Lieutenant Lord Louis Mountbatten, and he was second-in-command of *HMS P31*, engaged on the vital anti-submarine work. He was 18 years old now, and grown up; a tall, extremely handsome young naval officer with

Mountbatten in 1919

a good war record. The Admiralty decided that the next step for Lord Louis Mountbatten, as for other officers of his generation, should be a spell at university. And so, in the autumn of 1919, he was sent up to Christ's College, Cambridge, to finish his education.

3 In Time of Peace

At Cambridge, Mountbatten showed once again that his interests did not lie in text-books. He was a sailor, rather than a scholar. However, university did broaden his knowledge of life outside the navy. He went to a great many parties, joined in the college activities and, like many other students, developed his interest in politics.

Partly through his mother's influence, he had grown up with a broader outlook than many young men in his position. Though at Cambridge he took part in a debate opposing the motion 'That the time is ripe for a Labour government', he was interested in socialism, he had friends with widely varying views and he remained a progressive thinker all his life.

With his good looks, his easy manner and his lively mind, it was not surprising that Mountbatten made many friends during this period of his life. But the closest of all was his second cousin David, the Prince of Wales. To Mountbatten's delight, it was arranged in 1920 that he should accompany the Prince on an official tour in *HMS Renown,* stopping off in such places as Australia and New Zealand. The tour — the first of several — was a great success, and it cemented the friendship between the two young men.

Mountbatten (*right*) with the Prince of Wales on tour in 1920

Soon after his return, Mountbatten fell deeply in love. He had had plenty of girlfriends, and had even come close to marriage, but now, in July 1921, at a grand ball in London, he met the girl he was to marry.

Edwina Ashley was then 20, beautiful, clever, amusing — and the heiress to a huge fortune. Her grandfather was a brilliant Jewish banker named Sir Ernest Cassel; on his death, Edwina would inherit millions of pounds. But all that mattered to Mountbatten was her compelling beauty and her vivacious personality, which matched his own.

Attraction turned to love — but before Mountbatten could propose, his father died and grief temporarily overshadowed all other feelings. Then Edwina's rich grandfather also died, and suddenly Mountbatten, the hard-up Lieutenant, found that the girl he loved was a millionairess. Rather than be thought a fortune-hunter, he chose to join the Prince of Wales on another Empire tour — this time to India.

Mountbatten hunting on an elephant in India

He found India 'a marvellous country', though he was saddened by the problems of starvation and political unrest facing the people. He tried to arrange a meeting between the great Indian spiritual leader, Gandhi, and the Prince of Wales, but without success. There was little else he could usefully do as a visitor, except learn to play polo — a game at which he excelled — and miss Edwina.

Edwina was a forceful young woman, with dash and courage, and when Mountbatten suggested in one of his letters that she join him in India, she set out at once. And so it was in the exotic setting of Delhi, on St Valentine's Day 1921, that Lord Louis Mountbatten finally proposed to Edwina Ashley, and was accepted.

Their wedding in Westminster Abbey, on 18 July 1922, was the social event of the year. King George and Queen Mary were present, as were the rich and the royal of almost every nationality. After a brief visit to Broadlands, Edwina's beautiful family home in Hampshire, they set off on their honeymoon, first to Europe, then on to the United States of America. Dickie had obtained six months leave on half-pay from the navy, and they meant to make the most of it.

In America the young Mountbattens had the time of their lives. Their easy, friendly ways, coupled with their liking for parties and fun, made them immensely popular with the warm-hearted Americans. Whether attending formal luncheons in New York, or making home movies with their new friend Charlie Chaplin in Hollywood, they made an excellent impression as unofficial ambassadors for Britain.

In the years which followed his marriage, Mountbatten

The Mountbattens' wedding day

managed to combine two very different images. He openly enjoyed his new wealth, driving expensive cars, owning yachts and polo-ponies, and giving enormous

21

parties with Edwina at her house in Mayfair's Park Lane. Yet at the same time he showed himself to be more dedicated than ever to his naval career, working hard, rising steadily, and never allowing the glamour of his social life to affect his devotion to the job he loved.

Signals — the business of communication between ships at sea and the outside world — was a branch of naval work which particularly fascinated Mountbatten, and it became his speciality. He passed out top of his course at the Signal School, Portsmouth, and it was a great day when, in 1927, he was appointed Assistant

Mountbatten with his first Rolls Royce, a wedding present from Edwina

Fleet Wireless Officer to the Mediterranean Fleet, and he and Edwina prepared to set off for their first tour of duty in the Mediterranean.

Even when they were with the Fleet, the Mountbattens were able to live in much greater style than most naval officers' families. In Malta their frequent entertaining and the presence of their private yacht caused some resentment, and Mountbatten was not always popular with his brother officers and seniors as a result. However, his own abilities and tireless hard work ensured his promotion, and from Fleet Wireless Officer in 1931, he rose to become Commander of *HMS Daring* in 1934 and then of *HMS Wishart* in 1935. To the men who served under him his colourful lifestyle was no barrier; they were proud of their dashing commander, with his royal connections; they respected his skill, and they gave of their best to him.

At home, as well as at work, Mountbatten's responsibilities increased as the years passed. Two daughters were born to him and Edwina: Patricia, in 1924, and Pamela, in 1929. And almost as dear to him as his own children was his sister Alice's son — a slim, fair boy named Philip. Alice, who had been born deaf, became increasingly ill during the 1920s, and her husband, Prince Andrew of Greece, was unable to bring up the boy on his own. So young Philip came to spend more and more time in England, where he was looked after by friends and relations, in particular his grandmother, Victoria Milford Haven, and his uncle Dickie Mountbatten, for whom he almost took the place of a son. Philip grew up reflecting many of Mountbatten's own qualities — independent, courageous and passionately fond of the naval life. There was to be no prouder man in England than Lord Mountbatten when, in 1947, the nephew whom he loved and had helped to mould became the husband of the future Queen Elizabeth II.

Close family ties such as the Mountbattens' involved sadness as well as joy, however: in April 1938 Mountbatten lost the elder brother whom he had loved and admired since boyhood, despite the eight-year gap in their ages. George Milford Haven died of bone cancer, and his family were heartbroken. As always, Edwina gave Mountbatten her support and comfort. His devotion to his work, coupled with her somewhat restless nature, which often took her off on foreign trips, meant that they were sometimes apart from each other for long periods, but the bond between them was very strong. Winston Churchill regarded them as an ideal partnership, and there was no doubt that Edwina contributed a great deal to her husband's success in life, both as a public figure and as a private family man.

With the rise of the Nazi party and the fanatical Adolf Hitler in Germany during the 1930s, the state of Britain's defences became a subject of increasing concern to Mountbatten. He saw, sooner than many, that war was once again on the horizon. During his trips to London the luxurious penthouse flat, which had seen so many parties, became the scene for anxious discussions between military leaders and the few politicians, led by Winston Churchill, who recognised the German threat. One of Mountbatten's particular concerns was the need to build up Britain's air power at sea — the Fleet Air Arm — as a part of the navy instead of a branch of the RAF. This war, he knew, would be very different from the last, and he did all he could to prepare the navy's defences for what was to come.

4   The Sinking of the *Kelly*

As the 1930s drew towards their close, it became increasingly clear that Britain and Germany would soon be locked in combat again, on land, at sea and in the air. Amid the dangers and tragedies of the war that followed, an incident took place that was to catch the imagination of the British people — the sinking of *HMS Kelly*, Mountbatten's ship.

He took command of the *Kelly* just before war was declared, in September 1939. Newly built and smartly fitted, she was a fine, modern K-class destroyer, and her commander was justly proud of her.

The *Kelly*'s first mission of the war was a historic one; she was sent to fetch home from France the man who had once been Mountbatten's best friend — David, the former Prince of Wales. He had succeeded to the throne in 1936 as King Edward VIII, but ruled for less than a year before abdicating, in order to marry the woman he loved, Mrs Wallis Simpson, a divorcée who could never be Queen of England. As the Duke and Duchess of Windsor, the couple had gone to live in France. Mountbatten had been deeply saddened by the abdication, and though he had since grown close to the new King, David's brother George VI, he was glad to see

Mountbatten — Captain of *HMS Kelly*

his old friend again, and be of assistance to him.

'Keep On', was the motto that Mountbatten gave to the *Kelly,* and she lived up to it. Seeking out U-boats, the German submarines that constantly threatened Britain's shipping, evacuating troops from Norway under heavy attack from the air, dodging enemy mines and torpedoes, the *Kelly* kept on, despite several incidents — one of them serious — which sent her back to the dockyards for repairs. Her commander gained a half-joking reputation for being accident-prone, but his men took pride in his courage and trusted to his skill.

On 21 May 1941, the *Kelly* set out from Grand Harbour, Malta, on her most dangerous mission yet. She was bound for Crete, where British troops were coming under heavy attack. It was her job to prevent German reinforcements from getting through by sea.

As she approached the battle area, German bombers swooped overhead. Other British ships had already been hit, but there was no time to go to the aid of survivors; the *Kelly* was urgently needed to help in the bombardment of the enemy, while keeping them from landing any more soldiers on the island.

All that night the fighting raged, and when the dawn came it brought, not relief, but fresh waves of German bombers coming out of the sky. The Oerlikon, pom-pom and 4.7 guns of *HMS Kelly* blazed in reply, as the destroyer dodged and turned to evade the attackers above her.

At 8 a.m. on 23 May Mountbatten was one of those who saw the Stuka dive-bomber approach and release the bomb that hit them; then he heard the massive explosion as it crashed behind the engine room. Almost at once the ship began to heel over, the water pouring in, while he shouted, 'Keep the guns firing — we've been hit!'

Some men were dead already, others fighting to save themselves. Mountbatten found himself in the sea, and when he surfaced his beloved ship was almost gone. Fortunately one of her rafts — a Carley float — was bobbing nearby, and he helped to haul men from the oil-blackened water onto it. As the *Kelly* finally disappeared beneath the waves, he led her company in three last cheers for her.

If ever Mountbatten's courage and powers of leadership were put to the test, it was now. Clinging to their raft, waiting for the rescue that might not come, Mountbatten and his men sang songs — 'Roll Out the Barrel' was one — to keep their spirits up. They went on singing gallantly even when German planes returned to machine-gun the helpless survivors in the water. At last the destroyer *HMS Kipling*, from their own flotilla, came into view, and the *Kelly*'s remaining men, about half of the original ship's company, were taken on board.

Mountbatten assumed command of the *Kipling*, as captain of the flotilla. During the journey to Alexandria, under constant harassment from enemy aircraft, he went

The sinking of *HMS Kelly*

round comforting his wounded men, some of whom were burned beyond recognition.

The relief was intense when they finally reached the coast of Egypt. The ragged survivors of *HMS Kelly* were cheered by the rest of the Fleet as they came into Alexandria, and for Mountbatten himself there was a special welcome — from his nephew Philip, now a handsome young Midshipman in the *Valiant*, who was waiting to greet him with an embrace and a joke. Back in England, reporting on the Battle of Crete, *The Times* informed its readers, 'It is understood that Captain Lord Louis Mountbatten is among those who have been saved'.

To those at home, the story of the valiant *Kelly* summed up the spirit of Britain at war. It inspired one of Mountbatten's close friends, the writer, wit and actor Noel Coward, to make a film called 'In Which We Serve', based on the incident, and Mountbatten himself became a popular hero. The men of the *Kelly* never forgot his parting speech to them; it was perhaps the finest example of his special style, that blend of direct, informal friendliness with a stirring sense of pride, which became known as 'the Mountbatten touch'.

Speaking of their dead shipmates, he commented, 'If they had to die, what a grand way to go, for now they all lie together with the ship we loved, and they are in very good company. We have lost her, but they are still with her.' He went on, 'I feel that each of us will take up the battle with even stronger heart,' and ended by saying, 'The next time you are in action, remember the *Kelly*. As you ram each shell home into the gun, shout *"Kelly!"*

and so her spirit will go on inspiring us until victory is won. I should like to add that there isn't one of you I wouldn't be proud and honoured to serve with again.'

Today the surviving officers and men of the *Kelly* still meet each year for a reunion dinner, although now their commander, as well as their ship, has gone. In the dark days of 1941 Mountbatten's spirit, like the *Kelly*'s, was an inspiration to victory.

5 In Time of War

Mountbatten's first love was the navy, and he had proved himself a fine commander, but to the British government a man of his talents had other uses in time of war, and he was not to remain at sea for much longer.

In the autumn of 1941, following the *Kelly* incident, Mountbatten and Edwina went off to America again — this time on business. Edwina had thrown herself into the war effort, working tirelessly for the Red Cross and St John Ambulance Brigade, and she went with him to campaign for funds; Mountbatten was bound for the United States Navy Yard in Virginia, where his next ship, the *Illustrious,* was then undergoing repairs.

At that time the United States had not yet entered the war, but they were showing their friendship to the Allies with arms and support, and their co-operation was of vital importance to Britain. Mountbatten had always got on well with Americans. They liked his combination of British grandeur and frank, easy manner, and his popularity with them was to prove a great help to his country in the years ahead.

The news of his new appointment came on his return from America. Instead of going back to sea, he was to join Combined Operations Command. As Commodore he would help plan daring raids against the Germans in occupied France, with a view to mounting the full-scale invasion that would liberate Europe and win the war.

It was Winston Churchill, Britain's great wartime Prime Minister, who chose Mountbatten for the job. Churchill had firm faith in Mountbatten's abilities, and felt he should be given the chance to prove them. Others were not so certain. Lord Beaverbrook, the powerful newspaper owner, had developed a deep grudge against Mountbatten, and he seized the opportunity to condemn the new appointment, through the pages of the *Daily Express*. Youth and lack of experience were certainly against Mountbatten; at 41 he was much younger than most of those running Combined Operations, and he was not always willing to take advice from his elders, if he thought they were fuddy-duddy and old-fashioned in their attitudes.

In the long run, Churchill was proved right. Mountbatten's early work in Combined Ops, which included the planning of a highly successful night raid on the French dockyard of St Nazaire, earned him promotion from Commodore to Chief of Combined Operations. To give him authority over the army, navy and air force, he was appointed Vice-Admiral, Lieutenant General and Air Marshal. He was now one of the four Chiefs of Staff with responsibility for directing the war. It was a remarkable position for so young a man to have achieved. Typically, Mountbatten took a special pleasure in having become an Admiral whilst still younger than Nelson.

With the entry of America into the war, late in 1941,

Winston Churchill with Mountbatten

Mountbatten's skill in personal relationships again proved very valuable. At his headquarters in Richmond Terrace, London, he ensured that American and British planners worked closely together, and when, in June 1942, America was proposing an invasion strategy which seemed wrong to the British leaders, it was Mountbatten who was sent in person to Washington, to talk to President Roosevelt and persuade him to change his mind.

There were failures, as well as successes. One operation which went badly wrong, and for which

Mountbatten took much of the blame, was the raid on Dieppe. This attack, which was mounted on the night of 18 August 1942, resulted in tragedy. Of the 5000 brave Canadian soldiers who took part, 1000 were killed, twice that number taken prisoner, and many others badly wounded. It happened that Lord Beaverbrook was Canadian by birth, and he made sure that Mountbatten received bad publicity over the Dieppe raid.

Despite the setbacks, Mountbatten's leadership of Combined Ops was generally successful, and by the summer of 1943 plans for the invasion of France were well under way. They included such vital details as 'Mulberry Harbour' — the moveable artificial harbour which the Allies would transport with them — an idea which Mountbatten was quick to take up. He never lost his liking for clever technical inventions and bright ideas, whether his own or other people's.

Combined Ops was an appointment which made good use of Mountbatten's alert mind and organising abilities, and he enjoyed the challenge; by the summer of 1943, however, he felt the need to be in action again. It was time he went back to sea, he told Churchill.

But Churchill, once again, had other plans for him.

6 Supremo

The tide of war was about to turn in Europe, but out in South-East Asia the fighting against the Japanese was still going badly for the Allies. For the British, as rulers of neighbouring India, the Burma front was of the utmost importance.

The Japanese soldiers were a terrifying enemy. Taught to believe that their Emperor was a god, they welcomed the chance to die for him in battle, and the fanatics among them had no scruples about torturing and starving prisoners-of-war. As well as facing a brutal enemy, the Allies were suffering from disease, intense heat, and a depressing sense of being cut off from the outside world. It was not surprising that morale amongst the 'Forgotten Army', as they called themselves, was very low.

At Quebec, in 1943, the Allied powers met for a conference, and a fresh approach to the war in South-East Asia was decided on. A new command was to be set up, with authority over all three services — army, navy and air force — and American, as well as British troops. The man chosen to be the new commander was Lord Louis Mountbatten.

Although Mountbatten was young, he had qualities

which made him the ideal choice for the job — in particular, his special relationship with America and his ability to inspire fighting men with his personality and example. His deputy was to be the American General J. W. Stilwell. 'Vinegar Joe' Stilwell, as his nickname suggests, could be sharp-tongued, and he had no great liking for the British; he had closer ties with the Chinese, who were fighting alongside the Allies, under their General Chiang Kai-Shek. For Mountbatten, however, 'Vinegar Joe' came to feel both friendship and respect.

As Supreme Allied Commander, South-East Asia — 'Supremo' — Mountbatten was under the direct authority of both President Roosevelt and Winston Churchill. But it was his own abilities as a leader that would make the

Mountbatten briefing General Montgomery in South-East Asia

difference between his success or failure in Burma.

He began to tackle the problem of low morale straight away, and once again the 'Mountbatten touch' was put to good use. Standing on a table or box, the Supremo addressed groups of weary, dispirited men and put new heart into them by his presence. His glamorous image, his relationship to the King, and his reputation for skill and courage all helped, and, rather like General Montgomery, he had an actor's talent for rousing his audience. Getting a few laughs to begin with, he would go on to some plain speaking about the work they had to do, and end on an inspiring note. Many of those fighting out in Burma with the Fourteenth Army were Indians, or crack Gurkha troops from Nepal; some were from British-ruled parts of Africa. But differences of nationality were outweighed by the close-knit spirit which developed — a spirit which owed a great deal to Mountbatten's efforts.

On the practical level, Mountbatten set about reducing the high levels of malaria and other diseases, by introducing new health precautions and reorganising the medical services. He raised the standard of Intelligence operations. He improved the transport of troops and supplies, and ordered the Allies to continue fighting through the monsoon — the season of tropical storms — something that had not been done before. This meant that the enemy could not use the monsoon as a rest period, during which they could re-supply their forces; instead, they had to remain in action.

Slowly the situation in Burma began to change. The idea that Japanese soldiers were supermen faded, as

38

they experienced defeat for the first time. As their morale weakened slightly, that of the Allies rose — and the news of the invasion of Europe, in June 1944, provided an immense boost. For Mountbatten, who had done so much to plan the invasion as head of Combined Ops, it was specially happy news.

The war against Japan had still to be won, however. After the fall of Berlin, Mountbatten was called from his hilltop headquarters in Ceylon to attend a meeting of the three main Allied leaders — Churchill, the new American President Truman, and Stalin of Russia — in conquered Germany. There he learned, in the strictest secrecy, that the course of the war was to take a new turn. The atomic bomb was to be used against human beings, for the first time in history.

Back in the war zone, while the fighting continued, Mountbatten went ahead with plans to invade the Malay peninsula. Then came the horrific events of Hiroshima and Nagasaki, when the West's new weapon of destruction was dropped, devastating cities and killing and maiming people on a scale never dreamed of before. On 14 August 1945 Japan surrendered.

It was Mountbatten who officially received the Japanese surrender, in a formal ceremony on 12 September. It was a historic moment.

Once the fighting was over there was still a great deal of work to be done, and for this Edwina came out to join her husband. She was present at the surrender ceremony in Singapore, and then she dedicated herself to the exhausting, and often heart-breaking, work of caring for those who had suffered during the war in South-East

Asia — whether prisoners-of-war or civilians who had been in Japanese-occupied territory. As the Superintendent-in-Chief of the St John Ambulance Brigade, Edwina was well qualified for the task, but she was appalled by the condition of many of the victims. It was a harrowing time for her.

Mountbatten announces the surrender of Japan in 1945

The men who had fought in Burma were proud of their campaign medal, the Burma Star, which King George VI had struck for them. When, in 1947, Mountbatten received an earldom, he was to take the title 'Earl Mountbatten of Burma'. In this way, his work as Supremo would always be associated with his name.

Back in England in 1946, Mountbatten spent some time with his family, resting and recovering from the war. He was hoping to go to sea again, but once again he was to be prevented by a new challenge. This time, the King and the new Prime Minister, Clement Attlee, had chosen Mountbatten for the highest appointment that any British subject could hold — that of Viceroy, or deputy King, of India.

7 The Last Viceroy

'Come out! This is a marvellous country', Dickie had written to Edwina from India in 1922, when he was on tour with the Prince of Wales, and she was a debutante in London. Always eager for travel and adventure, she had set off at once, and in India the young naval officer and the rich society girl had become engaged to be married.

Now, twenty-five years later, they were to return to that 'marvellous country' as Viceroy and Vicereine, with the historic task of handing over power from the British crown to the people of India. It was probably the greatest challenge of Mountbatten's life.

His mother, Victoria, and many of his friends and colleagues were dismayed when they heard the news. 'How can you expect that the 1000 years' gulf that yawns between Muslim and Hindu will be bridged within fourteen months?' Winston Churchill demanded in a speech to Parliament. Everyone knew that India, once 'the brightest jewel in the crown of Empire', was now in a dangerous state of political unrest. Violence, rioting and famine were everywhere, causing great suffering; and the religious conflicts between her 400 million or so inhabitants — a fifth of the world's population — threatened the country's hopes of a peaceful, independent future. As the Mountbattens flew into Delhi on 21 March 1947, there could be no doubt that they were flying into a difficult and even dangerous situation.

Mountbatten was officially created Viceroy three days after his arrival, and during the glittering ceremony — almost a coronation — he made his position clear. 'I am under no illusion about the difficulty of my task', he told the listening world. 'I shall need the greatest goodwill of the greatest possible number, and I am asking India today for that goodwill.' In the weeks that followed, he was to gain the confidence of the Indian leaders and people as almost no one else could have done.

His energy and his skill in public relations had always been among his greatest assets; the fact that he was both a member of the British royal family and a believer in social reform proved a great help. It meant that while India was facing the biggest upheaval of her recent history, she was governed by a Viceroy who stood for the values of the past, but was known to favour change and progress. The Mountbattens lived in the height of regal luxury, surrounded by servants, yet their personal charm and easy, friendly behaviour made them popular with almost all who met them.

One of the most important men in India, Jawaharlal Nehru, quickly became their close friend. He was the leader of the Hindus, who were the majority in India, and his Congress Party held the real power in the country in 1947. His main opponent, who represented the interests of the smaller Muslim group, was called Muhammad Ali Jinnah — and with him Mountbatten

The Mountbattens' first meeting with Mahatma Gandhi

had less success.

The original plan had been that there would be one united India, in which all religious groups would live together. But Jinnah would accept nothing less than the creation of a separate Muslim country, to be called Pakistan, and so, in the end, it had to be. After endless meetings and discussions, the Mountbatten Plan was agreed. There would be two nations — a basically Hindu India, and a Muslim Pakistan, divided into two parts, East and West, roughly according to where the different religious communities were then living. This partition was by no means ideal, since many people were living in what would now be the wrong area for their religion, but Mountbatten felt that it was the best compromise that could be found in the time available. He was convinced that a speedy settlement was vital, if civil war was to be avoided. Independence Day was finally set for 15 August 1947 — just five months after his arrival in India. He ticked off the days on a calendar in his office.

Back in London the Prime Minister, Clement Attlee, announced to Parliament that complete success had been achieved in India. But he did not see the horrors of the rioting that followed the decision for partition, when Muslims and Hindus maimed and killed each other in

The signing of the Partition for India. With Mountbatten are Nehru (*left*), Ismay (*centre*) and Jinnah

the name of religion. The great holy man, Mahatma Gandhi, whom millions of Indians regarded as their spiritual leader, tried to impress the need for peace on his followers. But even he could not stop the slaughter though he was willing to go on a hunger-strike and even die in the cause. Independence Day came at last; the British officially gave up their power, and all India rejoiced and celebrated. But when it was over the killings went on.

As usual, Edwina did everything she could to ease the suffering. She had been a superb Vicereine, admired for her beauty and style: now she threw herself whole-heartedly into the work of visiting hospitals and helping to care for the sick and refugees. Mountbatten had been invited to stay on as Governor-General of India (though not of the new Pakistan), and there was no doubt that he owed part of the affection and respect which he had won from the Indian people to the impression which Edwina had made on them. Winston Churchill had been right when he described the Mountbattens as the perfect team.

Late in 1947 they briefly left their duties in struggling India to return to England for a family wedding that was also a great state occasion. One of Mountbatten's dearest wishes had come true: the nephew whom he had helped to bring up was to become the husband of the next Queen of England. As Prince Philip and Princess Elizabeth walked down the aisle of Westminster Abbey together, on 20 November 1947, 'Uncle Dickie' was both proud and happy. To complete his joy, his first grandchild, Patricia's son Norton Knatchbull, had been christened by the Archbishop of Canterbury a few days earlier. The future of the Mountbatten line, which meant so much to him, was assured.

Back in India the assassination of Gandhi, by a Hindu fanatic, shocked the world, and brought fresh anxieties to Mountbatten as Governor-General. But as the nation slowly emerged from her suffering, and the chaos died down, he began to feel considerable pride in his achievements as Viceroy. Certainly the Indian people felt a great debt to him. When he was killed, more than thirty years afterwards, the official mourning in India lasted for a week.

8 First Sea Lord

When the speeches and thanks were over, and the last farewells had been said, the Mountbattens left India and returned home to England in June 1948. Mountbatten was now 48, still in the prime of life, and, as always, he was eager to get back to sea. In spite of all that he had achieved during the past ten years, and all the honours that he had won, he had yet to fulfil his greatest ambition — his boyhood dream of following in his father's footsteps, and becoming First Sea Lord.

For a man in his position, a national hero who had governed millions of people, it would not be easy fitting into naval life again, and taking orders. The British government knew this, and there were several attempts to find other work for the ex-Viceroy, more suited to his high status. One suggestion was that he might become Britain's ambassador to Russia — but he reminded the Foreign Secretary, Ernest Bevin, that Communists had murdered his aunt, uncle and beloved cousins (the Tsar and his family) and the matter was dropped. The more attractive post of ambassador to Washington was also talked of, but Mountbatten would not be budged; before going to India he had had Clement Attlee's promise that he could return to the navy, in command of the 1st

Mountbatten was a keen polo player throughout his life

Cruiser Squadron, and that was what he was going to do.

The former Viceroy and Vicereine were delighted when they found themselves back in the naval life, living in Malta again. Late in 1949 there was a special pleasure in store — Prince Philip and Princess Elizabeth came out to join them in the Mediterranean, while Prince Philip was serving as First Lieutenant in *HMS Chequers.* It was a happy period for both couples.

In 1950 Mountbatten came a step closer to achieving his ambition when he was appointed Fourth Sea Lord. He had already held the title of Vice-Admiral during the war, when he was in charge of Combined Operations, but this time the rank meant a great deal more to him.

If anyone cared even more than Mountbatten about his ambition to be First Sea Lord, it was his mother. Victoria Milford Haven was now 87, but her husband's memory was still vivid in her mind, and she longed to see her son fill his old place at the Admiralty. For once, this strong-willed old lady did not have her way. She died in the autumn in 1950, and Mountbatten was deeply grieved. The loss of his mother was, to him, the loss of one of his dearest friends.

The progress towards the top continued when Mountbatten was appointed Commander-in-Chief Mediterranean, in 1952, and, for the last time in his career, went to serve at sea again. He had lost none of his old dedication to hard work; he enjoyed shipboard life as much as ever, and he still had a magic touch when dealing with the men under his command — although with his equals and superiors in rank there could, as ever, be difficulties.

With Winston Churchill his relationship since the war had been stormy. Some thought there might have been a touch of resentment on Churchill's part at times when Mountbatten seemed to be taking too much glory. What was certain was that Churchill, 'an Empire man to

Mountbatten — Commander-in-Chief Mediterranean

the last', had bitterly opposed giving independence to India, and had condemned Mountbatten for his part in it, even refusing to speak to him on his return. As Prime Minister, there seemed every likelihood that he would try to block Mountbatten's appointment to the office of First Sea Lord, and there were those within the Admiralty who would support him.

But Mountbatten had too much charm, as well as influence, to be kept from his goal for long. In 1955 Churchill and the remaining opposition gave way, and so, at last, Earl Mountbatten of Burma achieved his life's ambition, and became First Sea Lord. To set the seal on his triumph, instead of using the office at the Admiralty which recent First Sea Lords had occupied, he insisted that the one which had been his father's should be prepared for him. He would even be working at his father's old desk.

Mountbatten's four years as First Sea Lord were busy; they included the Suez Crisis of 1956, when President Nasser of Egypt closed the Suez Canal against its legal owners, France and Britain, and for a short time it seemed that British forces were about to become involved in a full-scale war again. Though Mountbatten personally disapproved of the government's actions over Suez, he did all he could to ensure that the navy was at peak efficiency and ready for action if needed. He had come into office with the intention of bringing the navy up-to-date, and by 1959, he had helped to shape a well-run, modern service in keeping with the needs of a nuclear age. After that, as Chief of Britain's Defence Staff, he completely reorganised the army, navy and air force by bringing them under one command — a major achievement. The man born in the first year of the century had always moved with the times.

Even in old age he enjoyed the company of children and young people, and got on well with them. Without losing his own dignity, he talked to them as equals whose opinions were of interest. His daughters, who became Lady Brabourne and Lady Pamela Hicks after their marriages, had ten children between them, and Mountbatten's relationship with his grandchildren was very close. In the summer he acted as host to the whole family at his Irish holiday home of Classiebawn Castle; there he and the youngsters would ride, swim and fish together, up to the last day of his life. The carefree atmosphere of these gatherings must sometimes have reminded him of those other summer holidays of long ago, when he and the Tsar's children played together and made plans for the future.

Among all his young friends and relations, there was one who held a special place in Lord Mountbatten's life — the future King of England, his great-nephew, Prince Charles. Having helped to bring up Prince Philip with such notable results, Mountbatten was often consulted over the education, and later the career, of Prince Charles, who nicknamed him his 'Honorary Grandfather' or 'HGF', and was devoted to him. The Prince grew up to share many of Mountbatten's interests, from polo to scuba-diving, and his decision to follow the family tradition and go into the navy was undoubtedly influenced by his great-uncle's inspiring example.

The death of Edwina in 1960 cast a long shadow over

Mountbatten's later life. She had always lived at a great pace, devoting herself to the causes which she cared about without considering her own safety, and eventually her health gave way. She was buried at sea as she had wished — a naval wife to the last.

Mountbatten was now a widower, and he missed Edwina, but he was determined to keep busy, even in retirement. He could not contemplate an empty old age.

9   Death of a Hero

As he passed into old age, Lord Mountbatten lost none of his enthusiasm for life. Honours and decorations — almost too many to count — had been heaped upon him, and he could look back with satisfaction on one of the most remarkable careers of the 20th century. But, up to the end of his life, he still welcomed new challenges.

At the age of 75 he even visited Russia, where he was given a warm welcome. He was one of Britain's most admired public figures, and as such he was much in demand, both abroad and at home. During the 1960s, when the Labour Party under Harold Wilson was in power, he carried out government inquiries into the important issues of immigration and prison security; the Royal Family looked upon him as one of their closest advisors, and charities and societies of all kinds were helped by his interest and support.

He enjoyed talking about the past, and he devoted a good deal of time to recording his memoirs for television. Understandably, he was proud of his achievements. Yet, unlike many former Admirals and Generals, he was no hard-line military man. In old age he became strongly committed to nuclear disarmament, believing it to be vital for world peace; in one of the last speeches of his life he addressed the Stockholm International Research Institute on the need for the great powers to abandon their nuclear weapons.

Despite the problems in Ireland, he and his family continued their annual summer holiday visits to Classiebawn Castle in County Sligo. The castle, which was built by Lord Palmerston, had been inherited by Edwina and the family had been holidaying there for thirty-three years; they felt part of the local community. The 79-year-old man who had survived the sinking of the *Kelly*, the Japanese menace in Burma and the political unrest in India was not easily scared. He did not even think it was necessary to have a heavy police guard around Classiebawn.

Mountbatten at the age of seventy-nine

In August 1979 the Mountbatten family gathered as usual for their holiday in Ireland. In the bay near the castle Mountbatten's boat, *Shadow V,* was moored — not a luxury yacht, such as he and Edwina had once owned, but a little converted fishing boat, suitable for family outings.

On the morning of 27 August a fishing trip was planned. Lord Mountbatten, his daughter and son-in-law Lord and Lady Brabourne, Lady Brabourne's 83-year-old mother-in-law and the Brabournes' twin sons, Nicholas and Timothy, aged 14, set off together for the harbour. It was a Bank Holiday Monday, and there were a great many tourists about, enjoying the sunshine. With the Mountbatten party was a 15-year-old Irish boy, Paul Maxwell, who helped to look after the boat.

They reached the boat, started the engine, and with Lord Mountbatten at the wheel, made for the line of lobster-pots — hoping, no doubt for a good catch.

In a car on the coast road two members of the Provisional IRA, the Irish political terrorist organisation, were waiting, with their hands on a remote control device. As the first lobster-pot was hauled up to the *Shadow V,* they detonated a bomb. It had been planted just where Lord Mountbatten was standing.

The blast which followed ripped the little boat apart, killing or seriously injuring all those on board and flinging them into the sea, some with their clothes torn from them. Lady Brabourne felt herself sinking down through the water; though badly injured, with a supreme effort she forced herself to think clearly, and not to panic and suck in water. Her husband, too, had survived the explosion, and so had their son Timothy. But the other twin was dead, and so was young Paul Maxwell, and the Dowager Lady Brabourne was soon to die of her shock and injuries.

Lord Mountbatten had been killed. If he had gone down with the *Kelly*, forty years earlier, it would have been a triumph for the Nazis; now his death in little *Shadow V* was claimed with pride by the IRA. By a strange destiny he was wearing one of his favourite garments, a jersey bearing the name of *HMS Kelly*, at the time of his death.

In justification for the bombing, his killers declared that Lord Mountbatten had been a military target, since he still held the title of Admiral of the Fleet. But the rest of the world could only feel horror at the murder of an undefended 'military target' aged almost 80, that involved the deaths of two young boys and a woman of 83. To complete the day's tragedies, eighteen soldiers were blown up at Warrenpoint in Ulster that same afternoon.

There was a great sense of shock and loss in Britain and many other parts of the world when Lord Mountbatten was killed. His name stood for courage and achievement; he had served his country tirelessly, in time of peace as well as in time of war, from boy-sailor to Admiral of the Fleet. He had moved with the times, and it was somehow typical of his blend of old-fashioned grandeur with a modern outlook that he, the great-grandson of Queen Victoria, the first Empress of India, had been the last Viceroy, responsible for giving India her independence. He provided a happy link between

The Royal Family attend Mountbatten's funeral in 1979

his godmother, that great Queen, and the young man whom he called his 'Honorary Grandson', Prince Charles, who represented the future.

The state funeral of Lord Mountbatten took place on Wednesday, 5 September 1979. Crowds lined the streets, and many more watched the sombre ceremony on television. Prince Charles read the Lesson, and photographers caught him wiping away a tear. He had

Broadlands, Lord Mountbatten's home for forty years

loved and admired 'Uncle Dickie', and he would miss his presence, perhaps even more than anyone else.

Broadlands, the 18th-century country house in Hampshire where Mountbatten had lived since 1939, was opened to the public shortly before he died. Today it attracts crowds of visitors of all nationalities, as does his grave in Romsey Abbey. Yet his true memorial is not in the place where he lived or lies, but in what he achieved and how he is remembered by those who knew him, those who served under him, and those who were inspired by him in the course of his long and remarkable life.

Important events in Lord Mountbatten's life

— 1900, 25 June	Birth of Prince Louis of Battenberg
— 1913, May	Enters Osborne Naval Training College
— 1914, 4 August	First World War begins
— 1914, November	Enters Royal Naval College, Dartmouth
— 1916, July	Appointed Midshipman
— 1917, June	Name is changed to Lord Louis Mountbatten
— 1918, November	First World War ends
— 1919, October	Becomes a student at Cambridge University
— 1920	Promoted to Lieutenant
— 1922, 18 July	Marries Edwina Ashley

— 1924, February	Birth of daughter Patricia
— 1929, April	Birth of daughter Pamela
— 1932	Promoted to Commander
— 1939, 3 September	Second World War begins
— 1941, 23 May	*HMS Kelly* is sunk
— 1941-3	Appointed Commodore, then Chief of Combined Operations; member of British Chiefs of Staff
— 1943	Appointed Supreme Allied Commander, South-East Asia Command ('Supremo')
— 1945, 8 May	Second World War ends in Europe (VE Day)
— 1945, 12 September	Receives official Japanese surrender
— 1945	Created Viscount Mountbatten of Burma
— 1947, March — August	Viceroy of India
— 1947, August — 1948, June	Governor-General of India
— 1947	Created Earl Mountbatten of Burma
— 1952	Appointed Commander-in-Chief, Mediterranean Fleet
— 1955, April	Appointed First Sea Lord
— 1956	Appointed Admiral of the Fleet
— 1959	Appointed Chief of UK Defence Staff
— 1979, 27 August	Killed